Grace & Mercy

Tracy Cooper

Copyright © 2019 by Tracy Cooper

All rights reserved. No part of this publication may be reproduced, distributed, or transmitted in any form or by any means, including photocopying, recording, or other electronic or mechanical methods, without the prior written permission of the publisher, except in the case of brief quotations embodied in critical reviews and certain other noncommercial uses permitted by copyright law.

ISBN: 978-1-7336754-8-2

Liberation's Publishing LLC
West Point, Mississippi
www.liberationpublishing.com

Grace & Mercy

Tracy Cooper

I came across Tracy Cooper on social media, and I would read his post every day. His words just made you stop and keep reading. His poetry flows and creates vivid pictures in your mind. You will enjoy this work!

-Nicole Mangum

"My grace is sufficient for you, for my power is made perfect in weakness." Therefore I will boast all the more gladly of my weaknesses, so that the power of Christ may rest upon me."

~2 Corinthians 12:8-9

Tracy Cooper

Accentuate the positive
Eliminate the negative
Believe God
Who is good
And not a man
Who can't lie
Who can satisfy
The mouth with good things
Only blessings without sorrow He brings
His praises sing
Because of the Grace and Mercy
And benevolence of the Almighty King
Creator of the Universe
Seek God and all else will be added to you
Do good and it comes back to you
Faithful the Father will prove
There's no secret to what He can do
He is able and on your behalf He will move
To His way stay true
He is amazing
Expect Excellent Things

Tracy Cooper
9/29/2018
Copyright 2018

In six days
God created the earth and seas
God cannot fail
And in the garden of Eden
Put Adam to sleep
And formed woman from a rib
God cannot fail
He fed five thousand
With a few fish and a couple
loaves of bread
God cannot fail
Many miracles
He has performed
God does all things well
In any circumstance
God cannot fail
He divided the red sea
To help the Hebrews
From the Egyptians flee
God cannot fail
He mastered these great feats
In all matters He does excel
He is omnipotent
He is preeminent
Lift Him up
He is magnificent
All sufficient
And able
More than competent

And fully capable
And for you to trust
God cannot fail

Tracy Cooper
9/30/2018
Copyright 2018

In a time of trouble
Right on time
When you're needing
A breakthrough
In your struggle
None like God is succeeding
A miracle you
Will abundantly find
God has not forgotten you
And in your situation
Your wilderness experience
There's transformation
Nothing can prevent
If you believe
If you have faith
God's intent
In your time of need
An Extraordinary turn of Events

Tracy Cooper
9/30/2018
Copyright 2018

Something happened
But I'm alright
Because God
Still reigns
I'm not collapsing
I'm doing alright
Because God
Doesn't let me live in vain
He meets me right where I'm at
And because I have faith
What has occurred has
no major impact
Maybe there was some pain
But God's spirit comforted
And consoled
Having His hand on me
The Lord encouraged my soul
His love is alright

Tracy Cooper
9/26/2018
Copyright 2018

Do the work
So that you may be found
Worthy
Be Holy
Peculiar
Be ever diligent
Stay faithful
Some may ridicule
And say that you're a fool
But let this be a tool
Your endeavor will be refueled
And your resolve strengthened
Don't be down
Nor ever demoralized
Just realize
Someone
Somewhere
Somehow
Is positively impacted
As mercy and grace
Has been enacted
Keep working
So that Jesus
By your efforts
Will be found
Your work won't be in vain
Valiantly your work maintain
A great reward will be obtained
Don't be afraid nor ashamed

Keep working
For you shall you shall wear a crown
In the New Jerusalem
Keep working
You shall wear a crown

Tracy Cooper
9/23/2018
Copyright 2018

Just Walking alone
Minding my own business
Not starting any trouble
The police pass me
And then they stop
They get out of the car
They approach me
They ask me
What am I doing here
I reply going home
I live on Elm
They ask me for ID
I give it to them
It checks out
They ask me where I am coming
from
Work I say trying to maintain composure
They proceeded to pat me down
I think I why am I being searched
Then it just so happened my manager
just happened to drive by
He stops and asks if there's a problem
They tell him don't interfere with police business
He tells the police that is my employee
Why are you stopping him
One of them goes and speaks to Mr. Handley
He tells them I am also his neighbor
And tells them he knows my parents
They let me go

Mr. Handley gives me a ride
I thank God for Mr. Handley
But I pray for the police
That they would not think
They're above the law
And don't have to play by the rules
Why am I a statistic
And why just because I'm African American
Must it be unreasonable or unrealistic
That in a nice area I reside
Why must that be reserved for only white men
I cooperated
I communicated well
Why was I detained
Why wasn't justice upheld
Justice the police did not serve
It was failed
There was no probable cause
The search was illegal
And uncalled for
My civil rights were ignored
This made me embarrassed
It was insulting
I was just walking

Tracy Cooper
9/27/2018
Copyright 2018

Love On Someone
Sunday is coming
We will gather.... Congregate
Fellowship as the Lord we celebrate
It's wonderful and fine
But love has no special time
Unfailing it's of the utmost design
It's flawless having all in mind
Amazing it's so kind
On a weekday be so inclined
To make occasion someone your heart to find
Love being your bottom line
On Sunday we love everyone
But Monday through Saturday
Plenteous let it overflow
A bounty to behold
Stingy let us not become
Be generous
Genuinely let go
Imitate Jesus
Into a soul this sow
So they reap its harvest
Liberally the precious commodity invest
Not expecting always to yield a return
For someone... Anyone... Be concerned
Honestly doing a good work
As you sojourn let love's flame eternal burn
Love on someone

Tracy Cooper
10/20/2018
Copyright 2018

We Are
Hopefully
We have a sensitivity
A typical tendency
An inclination to see
What we ought to be
God's destiny
Plan and expected end
A hope and a future
We are blessed indeed
Made wonderfully
And fearfully
By the Almighty
Furnished
And equipped
For every good work
A thing of beauty
Created supernaturally
Who in Christ
Can do all things
We are strengthened
And enabled
We cannot be unearthed
Inside of God's ability
We are a masterpiece
Literally
And we are
Capable of doing God's will
Efficiently

Daily
Obediently
Incredibly
Yes fulfill
On purpose
Intentionally
What needs to be
For such a time as this
We can run the race
Dedicated
Pressing
On one accord
Possessing
Integrity
We are vessels
Made to endure
Overcome
And more than conquer
Triumphantly
Exceedingly
But giving God
All the Glory
Author
And finisher
Of our story
We win
For God in us
Being
Final Authority

Of this be aware
Decree
And declare
This
Is who we are

Tracy Cooper
10/21/2018
Copyright 2018

Naked
Men
View
Visually
Having
The
Daunting task
To advert our eyes
Constantly
So we can
Avoid behaving
Lustfully
We need help
From on high
To exhibit
Self-control
Because
On fire
Is our soul
We want to
Be whole
Spiritually
But it is difficult
In the natural
It is easy to be
Caught up
For it is factual
That many of you
Who are of the feminine species

Don't mind
Appearing
In clothing scantily
You and society
Pop culture
Call it sexy
But the outer adornment
Should be seen
Modestly
Discreetly
A thing of beauty
Not a thing objectively
I know my responsibility
Wholeheartedly
To see you
To know you
Virtuously
Is how it should be
Instead
Of seeing you
Infamously
On social media
Practically
Nude
You always poke me
Indiscreetly
I end up deleting you
That part of you
I don't want to see

Naked

Tracy Cooper
10/21/2018
Copyright 2018

A New Community
A place far better
Which exceeds
Any far away earthly destination
It's celestial
Quintessential
Purely Paradise
Nothing can ever compare
There is never any night there
There's a crystal fountain
Streets of gold
And a mansion
Just for you
Built by a Savior
Jesus
No war
Nor crime
No prejudice
Exists there
Love in the atmosphere
Upon Jesus
All will be fixed
In this
The Ultimate
Eternity
Heaven
A New Community

Tracy Cooper
9/23/2018
Copyright 2018

Leave Him Alone

Leave him alone
Don't despise him
Nor judge him
Nor talk about him
Just pray
Love him
Stand by him
Even if others
Yeah including yourself
For one second think
He has gone astray
God isn't done
With him yet
He may not be perfect
According to your own ideas
And to others there may be no other appeal
Yet he is a creation by God still
To God he has value that is real
For me this is an epiphany
A sin of which I must repent
Yes just expediently atone
And more reverently for him pray
I will leave him alone

Tracy Cooper
9/23/2018
Copyright 2018

Thinking Of You
A reflection by
Meditation
Pure
Unadulterated
Remembrance
Of my king
Experiencing
Knowing
Golden
Beholding
All this
Fond reminiscence
Sweet
Holy
Incomparable
Thinking of You

Tracy Cooper
9/12/2018
Copyright 2018

A Knowing
I am feeling some kind of way
But it's only a feeling
A heaviness that wants to stay
Thinking a role it will make me portray
But that's not the way of the Almighty
The way of the Almighty
Is not flighty
For the outcome is secured
A blessing assured
Victory on one accord
I praise Him for it is He
That causes me to triumph
I will shout... I will not be silent
This feeling will not make be defiant
Its treacherous a tyrant
Yet I will succeed
Following the Holy Spirit's lead
I'm not trapped but freed
I have this knowing
Like a river flowing
A flower flourishing
growing
Fruit ripe showing
God into me confidence
sowing
This feeling
Isn't taking my healing
Not taking my peace

That to my spirit
God is revealing
Deep inside
It abides
I've got a knowing

Tracy Cooper
9/17/2018
Copyright 2018

You Shall Wear A Crown

Do the work
So that you may be found
Worthy
Be Holy
Peculiar
Be ever diligent
Stay faithful
Some may ridicule
And say that you're a fool
But let this be a tool
Your endeavor will be refueled
And your resolve strengthened
Don't be down
Nor ever demoralized
Just realize
Someone
Somewhere
Somehow
Is positively impacted
As mercy and grace
Has been enacted
Keep working
So that Jesus
By your efforts
Will be found
Your work won't be in vain
Valiantly your work maintain
A great reward will be obtained

Don't be afraid nor ashamed
Keep working
For you shall you shall wear a crown
In the New Jerusalem
Keep working
You shall wear a crown

Tracy Cooper
9/23/2018
Copyright 2018

Hear Ye
Hear ye
What sayeth
The Lord
Listen to hear
On one accord
Be still and know
Be all in
Be tuned in
Draw nigh
Don't deny
Because it may not satisfy
That which is carnal
That which is only quick to gratify
A soul infusion
It's a good illusion
Momentarily
Then it dies
Listen to hear
So that it's vividly clear
Perhaps from an unlikely source
The Lord is speaking
To guide you
Ordering your steps
Navigating you
On the pathway correct
The straight and narrow way
So that you avoid wrecks
Snares and traps

Study and show thyself approved
Be still and unmoved
The Lord is trying to get your attention
Pay attention
Hear ye
What sayeth the Lord
Be not too consumed
With the matters of this world
They must come to pass
Yes obviously they're facts
But to the truth hold fast
Only will His truth last
Hear ye
What sayeth
The Lord

Tracy Cooper
9/23/2018
Copyright 2018

Show Me Myself
To carry on
Make it apparent
My faults
My deficiencies
My weakness
So I can be transparent
Reveal
Clearly let me see
Insufficient things
Hindering me
Show me the person I am
So I can be the servant
That You want me to be
Righteously
Oh God make me over
Selfless and sober
A clean heart
Create in me
And a right spirit
Within me
That I should not sin
Against You
Doing your will
Willing and able
So I can live for You
Oh God your plan
For my life I fulfill
So openly and honestly I come

I say Lord have Your way
So the race I run
Properly
With all diligence
Order my steps
That I may walk
In a way upright
So Holy I will be in your sight
In the power of your might
In your awesome ability
So I stand victoriously
Lord You are my help
Please
Show me myself

Tracy Cooper
9/22/2018
Copyright 2018

Declaration of Love

I pledge
I promise
To love
Like Christ
Loved the church
Beholding you
And as I love you
I intend to put God first
As we enter our union
Remember
A threefold cord
Isn't easily broken
I will cherish you
My adoration is true
I will honor you
Respecting you
Listening to you
Sharing with you
Whatever we do
It will be pure
Genuine and True
Believe
These are more than words spoken
God gave me a blessing
To have and hold
A treasure
More precious
More valuable than gold

It's my mission
My prized possession to uphold
Inner and outer beauty
Is what you're made of
To my wonderful gift
This is my declaration of love

Tracy Cooper
9/13/2018
Copyright 2018

The Final Say
No matter what
The conditions
Or circumstances
God is able and faithful
This is but a light thing
Not catching the Almighty
By surprise
Whose report shall we believe
Don't leave it to change
His truth realize
Makes a way from no way
Never leaving nor forsaking
He will never deceive
Only up higher your soul taking
No heart will he ever be breaking
There is no problem unsolvable
He specializes in the impossible
God Almighty is unstoppable
And He is good
Loving your soul
Final Authority
He is in control
And has the Final Say
Just for you

Tracy Cooper
9/22/2018
Copyright 2018

Belong to the Day
The long night is ending
Surrender
The season of reckoning
Is about to come
Stop being an offender
Your sins will find you out
Light as bright as the noonday sun
Will uncover any iniquity
It's not too late
To be delivered
The best option
To avoid misery in hell
Repent
Change your ways
Belong to the Day

Tracy Cooper
9/24/2018
Copyright 2018

Far Away Child
Not meaning to be
Remorsefully
Upon a road
Carrying
A weight
Far too great
Burden of iniquity
In a state
I've fallen ill
Endless
Seems
This fate
Hopelessness
All too real
Not ever
Needing to be
Still I proceed
On the pathway
Wide and great
Contrarily
Outside of the will
I lost
I have to repent,
This route
I've come to resent
I made
An unfortunate choice
Becoming

An end result
Unrelenting
Very intense
Nonsense
I'm in motion
But stuck in neutral
Oh lord
Please forgive me
Upon me
Have mercy mild
Master
Once more
Make me yours
I need an off ramp
Make a detour
I don't want to be encamped
On this freeway
Futile
This straight
To nowhere
I now cast my care
I know longer
Desire to be defiled
On the Avenue of despair
Being a Far Away Child

Tracy Cooper
9/14/2018
Copyright 2018

Thank You Lord
Thank You Lord
My God
My Savior
My hope
My heart
Oh how I was
And in need
Of You
I had fallen short
Of your will
I'm thankful for
From where You brought
me from
Plainly sin
You have given me grace
You have delivered me
Uplifted me
Causing me
Not to be
Guilty
Once again
Without heaviness
I can run this race
And be of good report
And your will not abort
And my hope as I serve you
And stay true
Tell others about Jesus

Living by faith
The only thing that pleases You
Being on one accord
Being in a Heavenly place
Seeing You
Face to face
By You
Not being shunned
And You
Saying job well done
Thank You Lord
For forgiving me
And another chance
Giving me
Thank You Lord

Tracy Cooper
9/10/2018
Copyright 2018

Being With One
Honestly to be with one
And be done
With your searching
Being with one
Being in love
Knowing
You're never gonna be hurting
Inspired
To keep on working
To keep on growing
To be sharing
The harvest
Cultivated
The nurturing
The fruit
Of your labor
You savor
Satisfying
On your pallet
Valid
Legitimate
Real
Pure
God given
You know
Throughout
Your time together
You could never do any better

You are driven
What God has put together
Let no man put asunder
The pledge that you live by
One till to the other
Till you die
A legacy of love
Being with one

Tracy Cooper
9/27/2018
Copyright 2018

Believe
Behind the scenes
God is working
Invisible
Immortal
Smiling
No anger
What man purposes
For your harm
The Father
Will turn it around
Sight unseen
And make it good
He is watching
He knows
He goes before us
Making crooked road straight
With assurance
And favor
He holds our times
In His hands
Have faith
God's grace
Sustains
Perfects
That which concerns us
Trust
Have confidence
In God's providence

Although you can't see
Believe in Blessed Assurance
Believe in His goodness
For us He has favor
Be still and know
He has no shadow of turning from us
He will never leave us nor forsake us
Believe

Tracy Cooper
9/27/2018
Copyright 2018

Sometimes
Sometimes
I think on folks
And I know
Those who have departed
While there for a season
God knows the reason
Truth is
They're in our midst
To be appeasing
A perfect fix
For such a time
They encourage and edify
Yeah they build you up
Making your heart filled up
With pleasantries
Fond memories
Together you drink
From cups of hospitality
Some are distant
Some have expired
They loved on me
And my soul inspired
I miss them
That was a sweet season
For which God has a reason
I think on folks
Sometimes

Tracy Cooper
9/26/2018
Copyright 2018

Be Broken
Many many times we want change
But we go solo living in vain
Yet we go on trying to maintain
With an approach that is the same
To God we have complained
Want Him to stop the rain
We in our flesh wanna do the job
We want the problem on our own to solve
We don't want to let God get involved
Independent spirit
The wise counsel of the Almighty
Creator of the Universe
His instruction we don't want to hear it
However the end result is highly disappointing
Plainly there wasn't any anointing
To yourself the finger you ought to be pointing
God is so very smarter than any man
And for your life He has the perfect plan
Lean not to your own understanding
Acknowledge the Lord
And He shall direct your path
He won't let you fall or be abandoned
If you shall with Him get on one accord
To His way hold fast
Surrender
Let your heart become tender
So the Lord can be at the center
So His power and majesty enter

Put God in all things first
So all things will not be cursed
To God be open
Be Broken

Tracy Cooper
9/25/2018
Copyright 2018

Rearrange The Atmosphere
To any evil spirit present
In the power of God's ability
Command it to leave
Cancel the adversary's essence
Don't bow down to his schemes and trickery
Tell him in the name of Jesus you don't receive
Making declarations and decrees
So that the wicked one flees
Yeah so that he vividly understands and sees
That you are not playing around here
Let the word of God greatly abound here
Refuse to bow down
Let your faith in God make a glorious triumphant sound
Make it crystal clear
That you him do not fear
As you rearrange the atmosphere

Tracy Cooper
9/25/2018
Copyright 2018

Grace & Mercy

If there's no you
I could do oh so many things
But for all my achievement
All I would accomplish
Would be meaningless
If there's no you
Oh Dear God
I am able only
Because You are able
I could have riches great
But without your ability
I have no ability
Money answers all things
But you are my everything
It has no worth
If there's no you
I could own many possessions
But they are just materialistic
They are just things
They would bring no real joy
If there's no you
Jesus in reality
These things have no vitality
They are not worthwhile in actuality
They mean very little
If there's no you
Tracy Cooper
9/23/2018
Copyright 2018

Your Will
At first
My human side
Wanted something
I desired this
And I left you out
Wanting to be seen
Puffed up with pride
Elevated it
Higher
Than you king
With a material thing
I was overtaken
I was mistaken
Taken advantage of
By my flesh
My soulish realm
Overwhelmed
Consumed upon
My lust
That bubble
I had to let bust
Reestablish trust
I cried out
To you Father
My soul
Empty..... bothered
All an end result
Of being tossed

To and fro
My fault
Lost
Feeling awfully low
All because I didn't follow
Your will

Tracy Cooper
9/24/2018
Copyright 2018

Accept The Challenge
Odds
Seem impossible
But for the God of the Universe
The Almighty
Who nothing is too difficult for
It is but a light thing
He is on your side
And goes before you
Making crooked roads straight
Allowing you to avoid a doomed fate
You don't have to be crestfallen
Just as long as the Lord you're calling
Put your armor on
Let the word resonate in you
Apply and confess it
Your need God will address it
With faith being your testimony
And you will have victory only
For the Lord will fight for you
Doing what is required
Being inspired
Having the Holy Ghost fire
You will not tire
The Lord will take you higher
The battle belongs to Him
Do what the Lord would have you to do
And leave the rest up to Him
You can't do nothing but win

The Lord our God is with you
The triumph Jehovah will give you
There is nothing that the devil can do
So stand your ground don't be moved
There's no way you can lose
You are blessed indeed
You are destined to succeed
Into what the devil does do not too much read
The instructions of God only heed
He will help you at the point of your need
Accept The Challenge

Tracy Cooper
9/25/2018
Copyright 2018

Someone Else
Whose that I see
Who are you now
Who are you living inside of
Vicariously
So intrigued
So caught up
Anything brought up
Is addressed
By another you
Someone else
I wondered
Who you are all this time
Can't get through
Philosophies
And multiple
Identities
Characters
Social views
Obscenities
Concrete
Bulletproof
Talking to some other
Engaged in conversations
Historically true
Aloof
These people are
That you so love
That you impersonate

Have long since had their due
Through social studies
Is the only way I knew... them
And what they went through
You won't silence them
You make pretend
I never knew you
I am in the here and now
Wish you could be somehow
I will pray for that
Someday you would come back
That you would be done
Being someone else

Tracy Cooper
9/24/2018
Copyright 2018

The Unfortunate Plight Of A Bl

I saw her running away
Then I heard her say
"Call the police "
Her attacker pushed her down
On the concrete
Momentarily
She got free
Only to be slammed into a parked vehicle
He got what he was after... his phone
But much more was captured
Her self-respect
We had called the authorities
After she was pounded
She did something which astounded
She with a child of two or three left the scene
Now as I recall
After getting past the initial shock
I thought she may fear for her safety
For her life and that of her child
The unfortunate plight of a plight of a black woman

Tracy Cooper
9/24/2018
Copyright 2018

Quiet
The essence is sweetness
You can hear yourself think
Rest you can keep
Enter in
Peace
Study to be quiet
Searching the scriptures
Seeking God's face
Intimacy
Fellowship
Getting revelation
Gaining knowledge
Receiving wisdom
Anointing
Beauty
Quiet

Tracy Cooper
9/27/2018
Copyright 2018

Love Waits
There is season
And a perfect reason
It isn't proceeding
Anxious desire not heeding
Unto folly not leading
It is not receiving
It is true
From on high
It is blessed
Having no sorrow
Absolutely the best
Being present tomorrow
It endures
It is seasoned
It matures
Beyond compare
Withholding no understanding
Storms withstanding
Hardships able to bare
Able to handle any care
Resilient
It is eager to support
Won't mind being a support
In every aspect
It won't abort
To your interest it won't object
So in its time
Has its own rhythm

It isn't blind
No misgivings
No regret
A flawless design
It reflects
Love waits

Tracy Cooper
9/24/2018
Copyright 2018

Casualties
Everyday
Something occurs
Residual
Repeated
After effects
A haunting refrain
Impact lingering
Struggling
To recover
To cope
Dysfunction
Abusive fathers
Children
Who suffer
Pain
Physically
Mentally
Emotionally
In need of healing
Pray they don't act out
Addiction
Gang activity
Reflex
Reaction
Chaos
Disruption
Disrespect

Arguments
Torment
A war zone
Sometimes death
Tragedy
Against it pray
For them not to be statistics
Or to be casualties

Tracy Cooper
9/23/2018
Copyright 2018

Tracy Cooper

www.ingramcontent.com/pod-product-compliance
Lightning Source LLC
Chambersburg PA
CBHW060505080526
44584CB00015B/1562